30002

DEMCO

ONCE UPON A WORLD

THE LONELY PRINCESS
An Indian Fairy Tale

and also
RAPUNZEL

by SAVIOUR PIROTTA
and ALAN MARKS

SEA-TO-SEA
Mankato Collingwood London

This edition first published in 2008 by
Sea-to-Sea Publications
1980 Lookout Drive
North Mankato
Minnesota 56003

Printed in China

Library of Congress
Cataloging-in-Publication Data

Pirotta, Saviour.
     The lonely princess/by Saviour Pirotta and Alan Marks.
        p.cm. -- (Once upon a world)
     Summary: Presents two tales to compare and contrast, the first from
India and the second from Germany.
     Contents: The lonely princess -- Rapunzel.
     ISBN 978-1-59771-079-4
     1. Fairy tales. [1. Fairy tales. 2. Folklore.] I. Marks, Alan, 1957-

     PZ8.P6672Lo 2007
     [398.2]--dc22
                                                  2006053190

9 8 7 6 5 4 3 2

Published by arrangement with the Watts Publishing Group Ltd, London.

Editor: Rachel Cooke
Series design: Jonathan Hair

Contents

Once upon a time   4

The Lonely Princess   6

Rapunzel   40

Taking it further   48

Once upon a time

Mention the words "damsel in distress" and the first thing many people think of is Rapunzel awaiting a beloved prince in her lonely tower. This powerful image is at the heart of one of the most popular fairy tales in the world, the meaning of which is hotly debated.

Everyone is familiar with the basic plot of the story. A witch locks her adopted daughter, Rapunzel, in a tall tower. This happens at a time when Rapunzel is leaving childhood behind and many see this as the key to the story: the witch is not horrible but afraid that Rapunzel might leave her to marry a young man. The witch is like a parent who cannot bear to give up her child.

At the climax of the story the witch throws Rapunzel into a horrible desert and blinds the young prince. Again this perhaps has a hidden meaning—suggesting that young people have to go through a period of pain and confusion before they find their feet as adults. But the story has a happy ending for the two lovers, as you will find when you reread it at the end of this book.

Rapunzel is a German story and many similar stories are told throughout Europe. Our first tale, however, comes from India and has a rather different conclusion. It is loosely based on fragments of a story found in a holy book called the *Jaiminiya Brahmana*. The jealous parent in this version is not a witch but a powerful sage.

The Lonely Princess

Of all the magicians and sages who walked the Earth, Asita Dhamnya was the most powerful. With only one word, he could turn flesh into stone, fields into desert, fire into water. Everyone shivered at the mention of his name.

There was only one person Asita Dhamnya loved, and that was his daughter, a princess of rare beauty, who was as kind as he was cruel. There was nothing the old sage would not do for his little one: produce dolls from thin air, make water dance, even perfume the night to give her sweet dreams.

Like all fathers, Asita Dhamnya believed his daughter to be the most wonderful creature in all of creation. He guarded her jealously, for he was scared of the day she would say to him those most dreaded of words: "Father, I have met a boy. I love him." No man would ever be worthy of the daughter of Asita Dhamnya.

Now one day the sage bought his daughter a horse, a silver-white mare, the latest of many gifts he showered upon her.

"I shall teach you to ride," he said. Father and daughter rode out into the forest, but the young horse was skittish and broke away from Asita's controlling hand. The princess held on bravely as it galloped off, her father following close behind.

The horse came to a halt, neighing and
panting, in front of a broad, swift-flowing
stream. As the princess soothed him, she
looked across the water and saw a young
huntsman, bare chested and bow in hand.
Their eyes met for the briefest of moments
and the princess smiled.

Then her father came crashing through
the trees on his black charger. "My
daughter, are you all right? You had me
worried!" He took the mare's reins once
more and led her swiftly away from the
river. When the princess looked back,
the huntsman was gone.

But that
one look
had been
enough for
Asita Dhamnya.
He, too, had seen the
hunter across the
stream and his fears about
his daughter turned to panic.
No prince, no son of a rajah, not
even a hero from the realm of the
heavens was fit to marry Asita's
daughter, let alone a shirtless hunter
from the lower realm of Earth. So Asita
took steps to prevent his daughter from
ever meeting an unsuitable boy again.

The magician had at his command a vast army of winged monkeys to whom he had given the power of speech. He had them build a magnificent palace, its floor inlaid with gold, its ceiling studded with diamonds so that it sparkled like the night sky.

When it was ready, he ordered his
servants to prepare a feast: fragrant soups
spiced with cardamom, delectable rice
dishes, fruit, and ice cream to follow. Once
the food was spread on a table, he invited
his daughter to the feast.

"How curious, papa," said the princess as
they walked together round the walls of the
new palace. "This place is like a fortress: the
gate is so heavy and the walls so high."

"Such a building, my dear, will keep you
safe," Asita assured her. "No burglar or
brigand could enter it." He chanted a spell
to unlock the gate, and the two of them
passed into the palace and sat down to eat.

When they had finished, the powerful sage asked the chief monkey to show his daughter around. Once alone, Asita chanted a spell and, two floors above him, the girl felt the palace lurch. She was thrown to the floor. "Papa," she called. "Was that an earthquake?"

She rushed downstairs but her father had disappeared. She looked for him out of a window and saw him far below, his face pulled into a horrible grimace as he screamed one of his spells.

A powerful
wind tore
through the
hall, ripping the
cloth off the
banquet table. The
palace was flying
through the air,
blown up and away
by a typhoon rising out
of her father's staff.
"Help! Father, help,"
screamed the girl. But Asita
Dhamnya was too far below to
hear her desperate screams—no
bigger than a snail now, a ladybug,
a speck of dust…

"It is better this way, my dear," said the chief monkey as the palace came to rest among the clouds. "Up here, in the realm of air, you will never come to any harm. Your father had your best interests at heart when he imprisoned you in this palace. Come, let me show you the games room, the library, the kitchen, the herb garden. It is your father's most dazzling creation."

Dazzling or not, the flying palace was still a prison and the princess could not be happy within its bejeweled walls. Without her friends she grew lonely. She stopped eating and instead fed her food to the many birds that flew into the garden of her gorgeous prison, in particular her favorite, a honey-colored eagle.

The eagle used to bring the princess leaves and seashells from the land far below. In return, she fed it choice tidbits from her plate and whispered to the bird about her dreams of the young hunter.

The hunter, whose name was Gauriviti, had not forgotten the princess with blue-black hair and eyes the color of wild honey either. He frequently returned to the spot in the forest where he had seen her, hoping she would ride by again. The wise ones of the village scolded him for neglecting his duties. "Forget whatever is troubling you, son. Concentrate on your work."

The time came when Gauriviti's people
were to offer sacrifice to the gods, to thank
them for the harvest and to ask for their
protection. They sent the young hunter into
the forest, to fetch prey for the altar. He
went with bow and arrow—and with the
determination to prove himself a gifted
hunter. But he could not catch anything.
He'd come close to shooting a swan, a
snake, a deer even, but they had all escaped
with their lives into the forest's depths.

At last, from among the trees, flew an eagle. It was so close Gauriviti could not possibly miss. Controlling his nerves, he pulled an arrow from the pouch on his back. The eagle, honey-colored in the fading light, dropped onto a branch and drew in its wings so that the hunter could not see it among the leaves of the mango tree.

"My name is Tarksya."

Gauriviti hesitated, the shaft of
the arrow held to his right eye. Was that a
human voice he could hear?

"I am a magical bird. Spare me my life
and I shall make your most secret wish
come true."

Gauriviti lowered his bow. He could see
the eagle's beak moving as it stuck its head

out from among the leaves.

"And how do you know what my most secret wish is?"

"I can see right into people's minds. I can read your thoughts as easily as reading a parchment scroll."

"And what is my most secret wish?"

"You met a princess once. You wish to meet her again, is it not so?"

Gauriviti, lost for words, nodded.

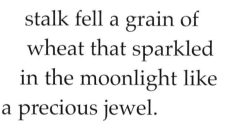

"She is the daughter of Asita Dhamnya," said the eagle. "Do not shoot me and I will take you to her."

Once again Gauriviti nodded his consent, dropping his bow and forgetting all about his people and his hunting.

Late that night, the eagle flew through the lonely princess's bedroom window with a leaf in its curved beak. The bird tipped the leaf over the girl's outstretched hand and out of its hollow stalk fell a grain of wheat that sparkled in the moonlight like a precious jewel.

As the girl watched, the grain grew bigger and bigger until she was holding in her arms not a seed or a gem but the handsome hunter she had seen in the forest. He was fast asleep, lost in a spell cast by the magical creature.

The young man opened his eyes.
"You kept your word, Tarksya," he
whispered, and the eagle cawed and flew
away into the clouds.

Gauriviti and the princess lay on her
silken sheets and the words between them
were as sweet as honey, as lulling as hot wine.

At dawn, the chief monkey knocked on the door. "Would you like breakfast, your highness?"

The girl, who had learnt some magic from her father, turned Gauriviti into a sparrow.

"Yes," she said, "I am hungry today. Come in."

"Who are you talking to?" asked the monkey, who reported all that took place in the palace to Asita Dhamnya. "I heard voices just now."

"I was only reading poems to the birds," said the girl, scratching the sparrow's head. "Put the food down by my couch."

At noon, the chief monkey returned. "Your highness, would you like a midday meal?"

"I am still hungry," called back the girl. "Come and put the food on the table by the window." And, before the chief monkey entered, she turned Gauriviti into a robin.

At sunset, the monkey returned to her chambers once more. "Your highness, the cook has prepared some supper…"

"Bring it in," said the girl. "I shall eat it on the balcony." And she quickly turned Gauriviti into a sweet-singing nightingale.

When the doors were locked for the night, the girl turned the nightingale back into Gauriviti. The hunter was so enchanted by the princess, and she by him, that the two of them swore never to be parted.

For many months, Gauriviti stayed in the
cloud-palace, letting his beloved turn him
into a bird every time someone approached
her in her chambers or the garden.

All went well, until one night, the chief
monkey heard muffled whimpering coming
from the girl's chambers. He burst in

unannounced and found the girl cradling a
baby, a child. With her was a young man,
the hunter from the forest, no doubt the
father of the boy. With a wild yell of fury,
the chief monkey called for his minions and
all at once the air was full with the beating
of wings.

The monkeys snatched the child from his mother's arms and hurled him out of the window. The chief dragged Gauriviti to the wall of the palace and  pushed him out into the void after his son.

Head over heels, the young hunter tumbled toward land, and certain death. Only, with each turn, he grew smaller and smaller until—on hitting the ground—he was no bigger than a grain of wheat. In the morning, Gauriviti awoke once more a young man.

Sobbing with grief for his lost child and beloved princess, he searched all over the forest for his dead son. At length he found his blue-tinged body in the stream, the dark weeds forming a cradle, a shroud, for the baby's broken limbs.

Gauriviti picked up his dead son and
cradled him against his chest. In his
sadness, he began to sing a strange chant,
one he knew had incredible powers.
Perhaps he had learnt it from the birds in
the floating palace, or perhaps his beloved
had taught him it in his sleep. No
matter where he'd learnt it, its
magic was working on his son.
Life returned to the crushed
limbs, a warm pink
replaced the blue
pallor on the
rosebud lips.

"He is alive,"
gasped Gauriviti.
He held the
child up to the
skies, praying
his mother
could see him.

He himself never saw the enchanted palace again, not then, not ever again. The power of Asita Dhamniya's magic kept it moving swiftly across the sky, so that Gauriviti could never reach it.

Sometimes, before the rains, he thought he could make out the faint shape of a castle in the storm clouds. Then he would hold up his son to the skies and shout:

"Look, my beloved. Your son, our Samkriti, is strong and well."

Far above, the lonely princess could see him wandering around the land. Sometimes, when the wind died a little, she would sing. Then Gauriviti would hear echoes of the song borne on the breeze, and know that his beloved princess was watching over him and his child.

Rapunzel

This version of Rapunzel *is based on Andrew Lang's English interpretation, published in 1890, of a tale by the brothers Grimm. Rampion, the plant featured in the story, is a salad vegetable whose roots and leaves can be eaten but is now more commonly grown for its pretty blue flowers.*

Once there lived a couple who had no children. They had a window at the back of their house, which looked into a lovely garden. The garden was surrounded by a

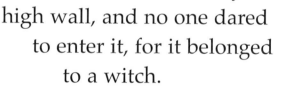

high wall, and no one dared to enter it, for it belonged to a witch.

One day the woman saw in the garden a bed of rampion. "If I don't get some of it to eat, I know I shall die," she said to her husband.

At dusk the man climbed into the witch's garden and, gathering a handful of rampion,

returned with it to his wife. It tasted so good that she just had to have some more.

So the next day, the man returned to the witch's garden. He got a terrible shock for there, standing before him, was the witch.

"How dare you steal my rampion?" she cried in a fury. "You shall suffer for your stupidity."

"Forgive me," said the man. "My wife saw it from her window, and wanted it so much I feared she might die if I did not take her some."

"If it's as you say, you may take as much rampion as you like," said the witch, "but on one condition—that you give me the child your wife will shortly bring into the world."

In his terror, the man agreed to
everything the witch asked. As soon as the
child was born the witch
appeared, and naming
the child Rapunzel,
which is another name
for rampion, she
carried her off.
Rapunzel was the most
beautiful child under the
sun. When she was twelve
years old the witch shut her up in a
tower, in the middle of a forest. This tower
had neither stairs nor doors, only a small
window high up at the very top. Whenever
the witch wanted to get in, she stood
underneath and called out:
"Rapunzel, Rapunzel,
Let down your hair."
For Rapunzel had wonderful long hair, as
fine as spun gold. Whenever she heard the

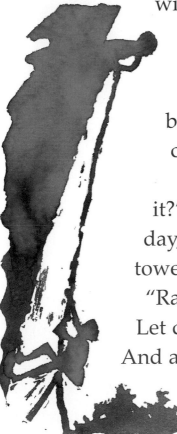

witch's voice she unloosed her braids and let them fall to the ground below. The witch used them to climb up to the window.

Now one day a prince was riding through the wood and saw Rapunzel at her window. He was about to call out to her when the witch approached and cried:
"Rapunzel, Rapunzel, Let down your hair."
Rapunzel let down her braids, and the witch climbed up.

"So that's the staircase, is it?" said the prince. The next day, at dusk, he went the tower and cried:
"Rapunzel, Rapunzel, Let down your hair."
And as soon as she had let it down the prince climbed up.

At first Rapunzel was frightened, for she had never seen a man before. But the prince spoke to her so kindly, Rapunzel soon forgot her fear, and when he asked her to marry him she consented at once.

"Every time you come to see me, you must bring a skein of silk with you," she told the prince. "I will make a ladder and when it is finished I will climb down so you can take me away."

They arranged that, until the ladder was ready, he was to come to her every evening. The old witch knew nothing of what was going on, until one day Rapunzel said by mistake: "How is it that you are so much

harder to pull up than the prince?
He is always with me in a moment."

"You wicked child," cried the
witch, "you have deceived me."

In her wrath, she seized
Rapunzel's beautiful braids and
cut them right off with a pair
of garden shears. She then
dragged Rapunzel to a
lonely deserted place, and
there left her to live alone
and in misery.

In the tower, the
witch fastened
Rapunzel's
braids to a
hook in the
window.

At dusk, the prince came to the tower as usual and called:

"Rapunzel, Rapunzel,
Let down your hair."

The witch let the braids down, and the prince climbed up. Instead of his beloved Rapunzel he found the old witch, who fixed her evil eyes on him. "You thought to find your lady love, but Rapunzel is lost to you forever," she mocked. "You will never see your pretty bird again."

In his despair, the prince jumped right down from the tower. He fell among the thorns, which pierced his eyes. Blind and miserable, he wandered through the wood, eating nothing but roots and berries. Thus he wandered about for some years, as wretched and unhappy as could be.

Then one day he came to a deserted place. Suddenly he heard a voice which seemed strangely familiar to him. He walked toward it, and when he was quite close, Rapunzel recognized him and fell on his neck, weeping for joy. Two of her tears touched his eyes, and in a moment his sight was restored.

The prince led Rapunzel to his kingdom, where they lived happily ever after.

Taking it further

Once you've read both stories in this book, there is lots more you can think and talk about. There's plenty to write about, too.

• To begin with, think about what is the same and what is different about the two stories. Talk about these with other people. Which one do you prefer?

• Retell the story, changing the men's roles with the women's. Would it work? Would it be more or less exciting? What changes to the basic plot would you have to make?

• Adapt one of the stories to modern times, perhaps as a comic strip. What kind of prison would the heroine be locked in? How would she react to her imprisonment?

• Write a report about every character in the fairytale. Try to find good and bad traits to point out. Can you explain why they behave the way they do, good or bad? Do you agree with their behavior? Discuss what you would do if you were in their shoes.